The Hubble Space Telescope: The History and Legacy of the World's Most Famous Telescope

By Charles River Editors

A Hubble telescope picture of various galaxies in the universe

About Charles River Editors

Charles River Editors is a boutique digital publishing company, specializing in bringing history back to life with educational and engaging books on a wide range of topics. Keep up to date with our new and free offerings with this 5 second sign up on our weekly mailing list, and visit Our Kindle Author Page to see other recently published Kindle titles.

We make these books for you and always want to know our readers' opinions, so we encourage you to leave reviews and look forward to publishing new and exciting titles each week.

Introduction

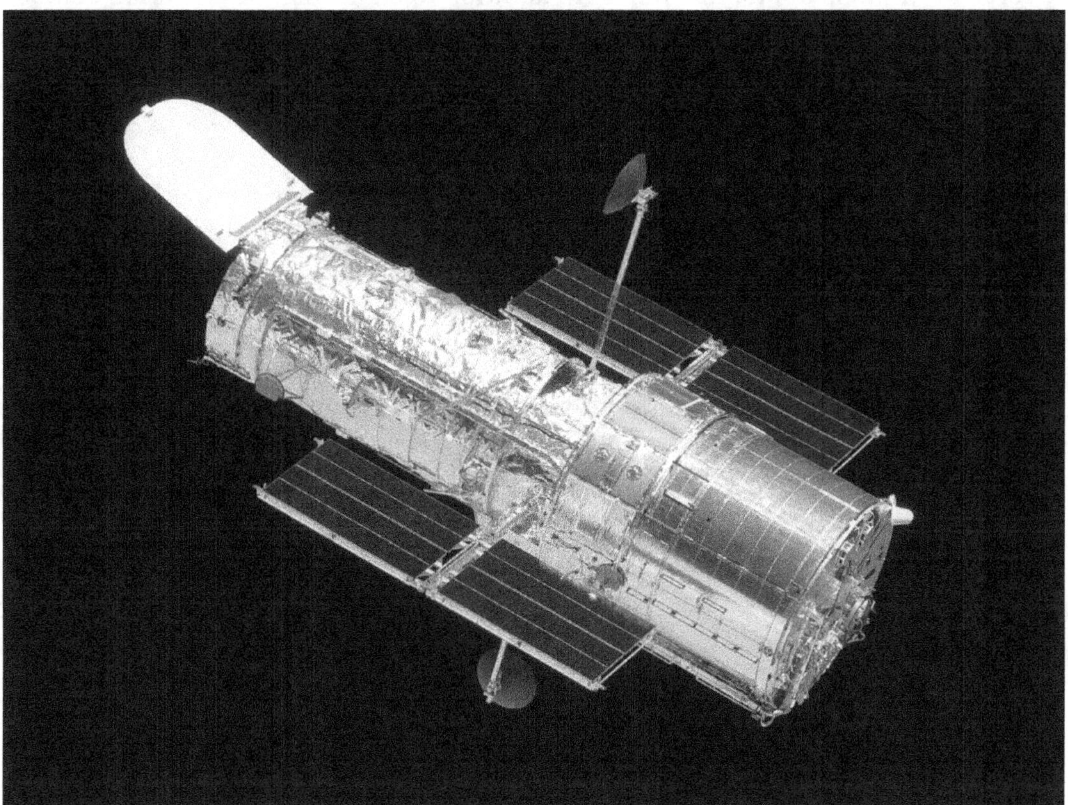

The Hubble telescope in orbit

On April 24, 1990, the Space Shuttle *Discovery* lifted off from Kennedy Space Center on the Space Shuttle Program's 35th mission, but this was no ordinary mission. In its payload bay, *Discovery* was carrying the Hubble Space Telescope, with the objective of putting the telescope into orbit.

By the time the Hubble telescope reached orbit, it was already the world's most famous telescope, but it was also the most scorned. The telescope cost nearly $2 billion more to complete than anticipated, and to make matters worse, the first images it sent back were skewed. When the telescope immediately began transmitting defective images, NASA and the telescope became laughingstocks, literally. In the popular comedy movie *Naked Gun 2 1/2*, released in 1991, one scene in a café shows a picture of the telescope between pictures of the Titanic and the Hindenburg, implying it was a disaster.

It would take three years to launch another space shuttle mission to fix the telescope, and that would be just the first of five servicing missions that have been performed in the 21 years the telescope has been in orbit. However, within about a year of fixing it, the telescope captured images of a major event in the solar system. In July 1994, the telescope provided a firsthand observation of a comet, Shoemaker-Levy 9, breaking apart and slamming into Jupiter. The comet broke into about two dozen pieces, some of them more than a mile wide, and hit the giant planet with the force of millions of atomic bombs. In addition to capturing the streaking comet breaking up and colliding with Jupiter, the telescope captured images of the impact marks that were left on Jupiter's surface, helping astronomers study Jupiter's atmosphere and debris left by major impacts.

Despite the costs and initial defects, the Hubble telescope has been a remarkably successful project, furthering astronomers' understanding of the universe more than any other telescope or instrument in history. During its 21 years in orbit, the versatile telescope has taken high resolution images of objects billions of light years away, giving astronomers a look at the early universe. Along the way it has also taken the most detailed pictures of the solar system, captured the most striking images of star creation and supernovae, and uncovered evidence of phenomena like gamma-ray bursts and dark energy.

The Hubble Space Telescope: The History and Legacy of the World's Most Famous Telescope chronicles the fascinating story of the telescope's origins, deployment, and production. Along with pictures of important people, places, and events, you will learn about the Hubble telescope like never before.

The First Telescopes

The magnification of objects, microscopic and at great distances, has inspired an inquiry of Earth's environment, involving creation itself. In the fields of astronomy and cosmology, four brief centuries have taken astronomers from small glass mirrors built by eyeglass craftsmen to sky-based telescopes, "liberated"[1] from the atmospheric distortion and background light of Earth.

Many milestones originated in 17th century Europe, a time of budding scientific frenzy, and the population at that time must have been awestruck by the introduction of lenses. Space devotees in the 20th and 21st centuries must be no less stimulated by the unthinkably powerful telescopes operating today in a low orbit around Earth. Early telescopes opened up space to the human race, whereas today's instruments can look back into time.

In 1608, a Dutch eyeglass maker, Hans Lippershey, patented a comparatively primitive telescope under the simple name of "*Kijker*," or "looker."[2] Some claim Lippershey stole the design from fellow eyeglass merchant Jacob Metius, who applied for a patent a few weeks later. Both were rejected due to a number of counterclaims and an official opinion that such a device was easily copied. Jansen went on to design the first compound telescope, and both he and Lippershey received awards for their work.

---

[1] McFadden, 2020

[2] McFadden, 2020

An engraving of Lippershey

   The Lippershey design came to the attention of Jacques Bovedere of Paris. He reported it to Galileo Galilei of Florence, who built his own telescope, and it is Galileo who has garnered the lion's share of credit for the telescope's concept. To be fair, the Galileo model increased the magnification of previous efforts by 20 times. With this instrument, he was able to draw the Moon's phases in detail, he discovered the rings around Saturn, and he could see four of Jupiter's moons. Galileo's design was powerful enough to detect a diffuse ribbon of light in the night sky, later identified as the Milky Way. Through his observations, Galileo was convinced that Copernicus's heliocentric model was correct, an opinion that caused him to be held under house arrest until the year of his death.

Galileo

Johannes Kepler contributed to the early 17th century with the Keplerian telescope. A German mathematician and astronomer, Kepler was an astrologer as well, before those fields parted ways in the modern age. Considered "the father of modern optics,"[3] he designed an instrument of two convex lenses, increasing the magnification but delivering the image to the viewer upside down.

Christian Huygens, a Dutch scientist, mathematician, and founder of the wave theory of light, used his own system to find another moon in 1655. The instrument was devoted to the study of the planets and solar system. Huygens introduced ocular and aerial (tubeless) telescopes and made early use of the micrometer. Assembling a 12-foot instrument, he confirmed "Saturni Luna," or Titan.

Sir Isaac Newton built the first reflecting telescope (as opposed to "refracting") in 1668. In his simple system called the "Newton reflector," a concave primary mirror was set against a flat,

---

[3] McFadden, 2020

diagonal second pane. The piece has become the earliest known functioning reflecting telescope. In his work with the light spectrum, Newton used what some have described as a crude spectrometer. However, the modern instrument was invented a century later by Gustav Kirchhoff and Robert Benson, and its ability to split light into constituent wavelengths became an invaluable part of space exploration technology.

Newton

Laurent Cassegrain employed another simple design near the end of the 17th century, called the "Cassegrain reflector," based on a folded double-mirror. Cassegrain was a Catholic priest with an ongoing interest in science and astronomy, teaching science classes in his late career.

One of the first large telescopes, measuring 40 feet in length, was built in 1789 by William Herschel in Britain. The largest in the late 19th century was built in Wisconsin as the centerpiece of the Yerkes Observatory.

The concept of a space telescope was theorized in 1923 by German rocket scientist Herman Oberth, who suggested such a "space-bound" instrument in his book, *Die Rakete zu den Planeträumen.* In the 1930s, Karl Guthe Jansky set about solving the static problems in the telephone system as an engineer for Bell Telephone Laboratories and discovered radio waves from the Milky Way.

   Sir Bernard Lovell conceived of an immense 250-foot disc radio telescope that could be aimed at any point in the sky. American Lyman Spitzer proposed it in 1946, and he lobbied for 30 years to manifest such an instrument. A researcher and professor at Yale University, he continued to argue the advantages of a space-based unit over ground-based examples. At Princeton, Spitzer headed the National Academy of Science Ad Hoc Committee and published the first paper based on a proposed project in the same year.

Spitzer

The New York Times (by Reginald V. Gray)

Lowell

By the time Lovell was working on his creation, the idea that a telescope in orbit would work much better than on Earth was being explored. In the 1940s, astronomers and scientists speculated that Earth's atmosphere distorted the ability of telescopes to take high resolution images, a distortion referred to as "seeing." This distortion is observable by anyone who stands outside at night and sees stars twinkling. In addition, Earth's atmosphere mostly protects the surface from infrared light and ultraviolet rays, which is good for life but detrimental for astronomy. Finally, all of the light caused by cities and life also affects astronomy done on the surface.

By the mid-20th century, technology had allowed people to create radios and other devices that could detect waves along the entire electromagnetic spectrum. Instead of just seeing light waves, telescopes were designed that could also pick up radio waves, measure radiation and thermal generation with infrared, and even detect x-rays and gamma-rays.

Building the Hubble Telescope

It was Lovell's dream that first broke through with a completed telescope in 1957, but 30 years of theorizing had not yet produced a delivery system for an orbiting instrument. The best Lovell could get was one of the most powerful land-based telescopes, situated in central England, but given that a telescope with all of these abilities would operate better in space, it was just a matter of making such a telescope and getting it into orbit. As rocket technology developed, the Soviet Union and United States were both able to launch satellites into orbit.

The year 1957 was an auspicious one, as the Soviet Union launched Sputnik, the first orbiting satellite. Little more than a 193-pound ball with a beeping mechanism, Sputnik ignited the fiercest phase of the Space Race between the Cold War superpowers. The United States launched its first satellite into orbit only three months later, and NASA was established on October 1, 1958.

The first meeting of Spitzer's committee was held in 1966 as a study of the telescope's possible uses. In 1969, the panel published *Scientific Uses of the Large Space Telescope,* urging that the design and construction of a prototype begin. For this to occur, support from NASA was obligatory. Wernher von Braun, the former Nazi official who became NASA's foremost rocket scientist, had considered the possibilities and recommended a small mirror of 120 inches.

In 1971, George Lowe, then acting administrator at NASA, gave approval to the Large Space Telescope Steering Committee for a series of feasibility studies. At that point, the process of fundraising could begin. Unfortunately, the price was a hefty one at $400 million, a tough sell for a country recovering from World War II and Korea while waging a "police action" in Vietnam. The recent Apollo missions to the Moon had been inspiring, but the costs were not. The request for funding was denied by the House Sub-Committee in 1975, but the ensuing partnership with the European Space Agency proved a diplomatic boon, lowering the overall cost. Following a mirror reduction from the original three meters to 2.4, the financial burden was halved, and the amount of $200 million was passed by Congress in 1977.

The initial progress on Hubble's construction was quick. A contract was awarded to Perkin-Elmer to construct the mirror and optical assembly, and grinding of the primary mirror began in December of 1978 in Danbury, Connecticut. Lockheed Missiles and Space Company, located in Sunnyvale, California, was engaged to build the spacecraft and all support systems. By the next year, future maintenance issues once the telescope was in orbit were anticipated, and training missions began for repairs, replacements, and updates for all components.

Computer-based lens-grinding provided a mirror so fine that a world-sized version would have no flaw above six inches, but when an optimistic launch date of 1983 was announced, it was subsequently interrupted by several factors. The first was an incomplete optical assembly, despite completion of the mirror, so the timeline was pushed further back to 1984. That date was not met, as optical issues took another five years to resolve. Another launch was set for 1986, but on January 28 of that year, the *Challenger* shuttle disaster halted the program for a period of two years.

A picture of the grinding of the mirror

A backup mirror produced by Kodak

The Hubble Space Telescope would not be the only space-based telescope, but the limitations of similar projects were exposed by Hubble's abilities. The telescope was appropriately named for Edwin Hubble, a leading observational cosmologist of the 20th century who all but established the field of observational extragalactic astronomy. Like his namesake telescope, Hubble "changed the way we thought of the universe forever."[4] With a Ph.D. in astronomy at Chicago University, he was invited by George Ellery Hale, founder of the Mount Wilson Observatory in Pasadena, California, to join the staff. The invitation came as Hubble was putting the finishing touches on his thesis and preparing for an oral examination. Hubble's telegram to Hale was surprising: "Regret cannot accept your invitation. Am off to war."[5] He enlisted in the infantry, returned to the U.S. five years later, and eventually found his way to Mount Wilson.

---

[4] "The Man," 2012

[5] "Hubble Overview," 2020

Hubble

   Four years after his return, Hubble observed what he believed was a nova star flaring in the Andromeda Nebula. He later realized he had seen a "variable star,"[6] officially known as a "Cepheid" that could be used to measure distance. From that point, he began a study of nebulae, and within a few years, Hubble realized that the universe was expanding at a high rate of speed. This resulted in what came to be called Hubble's Law. It is, in effect, a statement of "direct correlation between the distance to a galaxy and its recessional velocity as determined by the red shift."[7] Hubble assisted in the design and construction of the Hale 200-inch telescope on Palomar Mountain, and he was the first individual to use the instrument.

   The European Space Agency contributed important technology to the long-struggling project, including the Faint Object Camera, the first two solar wings that power the craft, and an

[6] "Hubble Overview," 2020

[7] Nave, 2005

excellent team of scientists and engineers at the Space Telescope Science Institute in Baltimore, Maryland. Since Hubble's launch, Europe has been given 15% of the telescope's observation time. The Hubble Project's European Science Archive is located at the European Space Astronomy Centre [sic] (ESAC) near the city of Madrid. Up to 2012, it was hosted by the Space Telescope European Coordinating Facility of the European Southern Observatory near Munich. The Space Telescope Science Institute selects the telescope's targets and processes the data from the Johns Hopkins University's Homewood Campus in Baltimore. All control of the aircraft is handled at the Goddard Space Flight Center in Maryland.

The case for a space-based observatory is by now clear to anyone involved in the ground-based telescope industry or any student of astronomy. Light traversing the known universe, seen billions of years into its journey, is distorted, interacting with Earth's atmosphere, like viewing an object through a vessel of water. Such distortions can be seen in the "twinkling" of the stars. Not only does a space telescope eliminate distortions, but in Hubble's case, the viewing spectrum from infrared through visible and ultraviolet wavelengths is available.

A picture of construction on the Hubble telescope

On April 24, 1990, the shuttle *Discovery* soared to an altitude of 600 kilometers to ensure a suitable orbit, a shuttle record. An iconic NASA photograph shows Hubble being suspended above *Discovery*'s cargo bay, 332 nautical miles above the Earth. The orbit is circular, at a path of 557 kilometers and inclined at 28.5 degrees to the equator. The Canadian-built Remote

Manipulation System Arm (RMS) held the unit in position throughout pre-deployment, which included the extension of solar panels and antennae. Deployment began the following day.

At the heart of the Hubble Space Telescope is the primary mirror, 2.4 meters in diameter, giving light to five scientific instruments from the optic spectrum. Hubble carries three cameras, the Wide Field Camera 3, the Advanced Survey Camera, and a Near Infrared Camera. The two advanced spectrographs are the Imaging and Cosmic Origins Spectrographs.

The Wide Field and Planetary Camera is a versatile instrument with which to image celestial objects over a wide wavelength and vast viewing range. From ground-based amateur telescopes to the Hubble itself, such technology is the "easiest way to get started in capturing photos of the night sky."[8]

Increasingly, advanced cameras have been built for Hubble in a series. The Wide Field Camera and Planetary Camera 3 (WFPC 3) devotes one channel for the ultra-violet and visible wavelength. A second is reserved for the infrared camera, covering a wide range of the optic spectrum. The sensitive detectors are solid-state, the same as in most digital cameras. For the visible spectrum, a silicon-based CCD camera, a video instrument with a charged-couple device or a transistorized light sensor on an integrated circuit, is used. A CCD camera is a video instrument which, in plainest terms, "manipulates an electrical signal into some kind of output."[9] However, in Hubble's case, that's where the similarity ends. The WFCP3 features 16 megapixels and a high sensitivity, low noise array. It was jointly developed by the Goddard Space Flight Center of NASA and the Space Telescope and Science Institute in Baltimore.

The Advanced Survey Camera in the latter series is a replacement for the original Faint Object Camera, installed during the third servicing mission. As faithful and as accurate as the original instrument, the Advanced Survey Camera accesses a wide field of view nearly twice that of even the second Wide Field and Planetary Camera. The addition has increased Hubble's potential for new discoveries ten times over. It captures large areas of the sky in detail while performing spectroscopy with a special tool called the "Grism"—a combination prism and grating—through which only the preferred wavelength can pass.

The Advanced Survey Camera operates three sub-instruments. Besides the Wide Field Camera, which can find distant objects and analyze how the universe evolved, the Survey Camera contains a high-resolution channel. Normally, this channel can detect detailed light from the centers of galaxies in which massive black holes are present. It is able to perform the same function with ordinary galaxies, star clusters, and gaseous nebulae where unseen planetary systems can hide. The Hubble's contrast near bright objects is improved by a factor of ten. In addition, the "Solar Blind" blocks visible light to discern faint ultra-violet radiation. In its

---

[8] "Wide Field," 2013

[9] "CCD Cameras," 2021

versatility, High-Resolution can study weather patterns on other planets or auroras, such as the type explored on Jupiter.

The Near Infrared Camera is employed to find extremely distant galaxies not seen within the visible range of the spectrum. Light received from remote galaxies has been stretched from the visible to the infrared by the expansion of space, and some has been absorbed by intergalactic hydrogen. Infrared capability has been essential to assembling the Ultra Deep Field Survey, a composite image of numerous observations taken through the years, giving a deep, narrow view of the cosmos, likened to "looking through a 2.5-meter straw."[10]

Coupled with the Near Infrared Camera is the Multiple Object Spectrometer. Light can be detected between 800-2500 nanometers and can penetrate dust clouds obscured by nebulae. The combined unit is called NICMOS.

The NICMOS must operate in a dark and cold environment, and scientists must ensure that distant light is being recorded and not the component's own heat. The infrared and multi-object spectrometers are maintained at -321 Fahrenheit, or 77 degrees Kelvin. In the first years, it sat within a thermos-like cryogenic chamber. Where one might expect advanced technology to manage the cooling process, an old-fashioned block of nitrogen ice weighing 230 pounds was used instead. The cryo-cooler performing the process operated much like a typical household refrigerator. A great deal of the work done by NICMOS has been taken over by the third Wide Field and Planetary Camera, but the future of the early component is undecided, as the WFPC 3 is not immune to malfunction. NASA anticipates it can eventually reach galaxies formed less than 400 million years after the Big Bang.

If such feats of optical wizardry are to succeed, some mechanism is required to hold the entire craft and its telescope utterly still to image such distances with long exposures. Another array of instruments, like those of the Advanced Survey Camera, can perform necessary functions and scientific observation and analysis at the same time. What is called the "Fine Guidance Sensors" give the general craft needed stability while providing information for targeting distant celestial objects and measurements of allied time and distance. The "Fine Guidance Sensors" are comprised of a large structure housing a collection of mirrors, lenses, servos, prisms, beam-splinters, and photomultiplier tools.

Sensors serve to maneuver the telescope for celestial measurement. Two are devoted to pointing the lens at its target, while the third makes myriad observations. One can only imagine the difficulty of setting a stable position within a floating environment, especially when the unit is approximately the size of a school bus and its camera the size of a baby grand piano. Hubble is free to roll easily on its optical axis, not in an end-to-end fashion, but as a log roll. Movement is

---

[10] Thomspon, 2021

somewhat limited by the need to keep sunlight shining on the solar arrays.

Sensors detect the slightest drift of the unit, even in the most minuscule amounts, and immediately reset the original position. So successful are these interacting mechanisms that Hubble's stability factor has been likened to holding a laser beam "on a dime 400 miles away for 24 hours."[11]

When employed in a scientific role, a sensor can search for wobble that signals an object is in orbit. It can identify a double star, measure a star's angular diameter, and refine the positions and brightness scale for any celestial object. In terms of measurement, it can determine the true distance scale for the universe.

Through its ability to separate light, the spectrograph reveals the chemical composition, temperatures, and motions of various planets, comets, stars, interstellar gas, and galaxies. In a unique process, light enters through a long slit, and before reaching the grating, the separated spectrum can be simultaneously recorded along each of the 1.023-pixel rows of the detector. If the slit is oriented across the nucleus of a galaxy, Hubble can measure how fast a galaxy rotates at various distances from its center. At the core of galaxies in which massive black holes reside, the spectrograph has uncovered and measured the mass of several dozen.

The STIS has been employed in the ongoing survey of gas and dust blown by unstable massive binary star Etz Carinae, residing in our stellar neighborhood, approximately 8,000 light years away. In the case of planet HD 1897, the spectrograph was able to determine the entire body's blue color in the visible spectrum. The spectra of transiting star HD 209458 resulted in light curves so precise the unit could detect the amount of starlight absorbed by the planet's atmosphere, and for the first time, a planetary atmosphere was identified as being comprised of hydrogen, oxygen, and sodium.

The STIS complements the Cosmic Origin Spectrograph, an instrument performing high sensitivity medium and low spectroscopy of astronomical objects in the 815-3200 Å wavelength range. The Cosmic Origin Spectrograph enhances Hubble's opportunity to seek out and image faint sources of light impossible to access from the ground. It is built to study large-scale structures in the universe, specializing in the evolution of galaxies, the origins of stellar and planetary systems, and the cold interstellar medium. Where the STIS spectrograph is an "all-purpose"[12] component handling bright objects well, the Cosmic Origin Spectrograph (COS) measures unthinkably faint levels of ultra-violet light from cosmic sources such as quasars.

Much has been written of the astonishing level of electronics among Hubble's varied components, housed in a protective shell, covered with blanketing material for protection against

---

[11] "The Telescope," 2021
[12] "Hubble Space-Telescope," 2019

a sinister list of dangers, even in a low Earth orbit. The New Outer Blanket Layers, or NOBLs, have "taken the brunt"[13] of the worst abuses of space, including severe temperature swings, solar radiation, and micro-meteoroids slowly degrading the cover material. Fortunately, most of the wear throughout the first years was cosmetic. The first servicing mission found the exterior pristine, but upon next inspection, nearly 100 cracks over five inches in length had appeared, and no one was certain when the next visit might be scheduled. To protect the exterior from daily bombardment, four patches of aluminized single-sheet Teflon were applied and are still in place. In caring for the shell, astronauts have learned much about space degradation and the general rate of decay, applicable to other missions. Among these concerns lies the reality of inner danger— wherever there are active electronics, there is heat generation and rising interior temperatures. Some of the blankets installed enable inner-cooling with a built-in radiator.

An array of elaborate altitude controls improves the stability of the instrument while it goes about its work. In terms of the craft's maneuverability, thrusters are entirely absent. Fear of contaminating observations is a serious consideration, as is Hubble's general lifespan. Heatless reaction wheels maneuver the Hubble into position, while gyroscopes monitor its movement for accuracy. The wheels depend on the "elegant" principle of Newton's third law; thus, "if one of the wheels turns clockwise, Hubble will turn counterclockwise."[14] Finally, the "Fine Guidance" sensors lock onto "guide stars" for accuracy.

■■

Fixing the Telescope
On May 20, 1990, less than a month after Hubble's deployment, the mission suffered its first unexpected snag. The inaugural target was prepared, and Hubble was producing images and data, but scientists noticed the mirror was "slightly misshapen,"[15] and an unfocused, blurry aberration was created in the images. At the time of its deployment, no one realized the mission was already in trouble.

Astronomers doing work in the visible spectrum anxiously awaited data and images, relying on enhanced clarity obtained from outside the atmosphere. 15 years had been spent designing the Wide Field and Planetary Cameras, and scientists and the general population were rapt by the story, waiting to see if Hubble could be salvaged. NASA itself had invested over $15 billion and would have been pressed to overcome such an expensive hit to its telescope program.

Ultimately, the fault was found in the fine grinding of the primary mirror, and as it turned out, the mistake had been made in 1981, nine years before launch. In short, a part of the telescope was near sighted. The repair would not be difficult, but executing it pushed the limits of

---

[13] Paquin, 2008

[14] ESA/Hubble, Kornmesser, and Calçada, 2018

[15] Smith, 2018

accuracy. "The solution for a nearsighted telescope is the same for a nearsighted person,"[16] explained Kiona Smith of Forbes, and that is corrective lenses. In a complicated and intricate process, five pairs of adjustable mirrors were prepared to refocus light from the primary mirror before it reached the telescope's scientific instruments. Throughout the halls of the agency, the most dreaded words - "spherical aberration" - were frequently spoken.

NASA was clearly in trouble, and much rode on the fate of a successful repair. Hubble's press was unflattering at the time of the launch, but it had only gotten worse over the subsequent three years. So much had been risked on the project, similar programs were being dropped at an alarming rate, and charges of incompetence were levied in the press. The *New York Times* asserted that had the mirror contract been awarded to Kodak-Iter, the problem would have been caught in time. The Space Shuttle Program itself survived Congress by one vote, and the "Moon to Mars" project ended.

Astronauts charged with the repair were aware of their job's critical nature. If they failed, political will for the Hubble Program would die out. The Mars Observer mission failed short of reaching the red planet, and rumors circulated that the Hubble's WFPC 2 might be faulty. President Clinton privately informed NASA that further failure would cause the agency to be restructured. From the shuttle to the robot arm, astronauts were required to work "with the synergy of a ballet."[17]

What Smith referred to as the "contraption"[18] was officially called the Corrective Optics Space Telescope Axial Replacement, or COSTAR. What the media had playfully referred to it as Hubble's "spectacles"[19] came with a $50,000,000 price tag. Everyone wanted to go up, but leadership was offered to astronaut Story Musgrave, a veteran of several missions and spacewalks. An obvious choice, his intense training prodded colleagues to joke that the only peace he could find was in the dentist's chair.

COSTAR's mirrors, each the size of a nickel, had to be perfected within three years, as did the new camera for compensating for the error. The Hubble's repair took on the reputation of a daredevil circus act, and at the time, it seemed that no one believed it could be done, and the agency had too much "Hubble trouble."[20] NASA became fodder for late-night comedians, and the once anonymous camera engineers lived in a public fishbowl. To some, the idea of making the camera out-of-focus in an identical manner to the mirror seemed absurd.

NASA took three years to build the correction, and when the shuttle *Atlantis* roared toward the

---

[16] Smith, 2018
[17] Evans, 2020
[18] Smith, 2018
[19] Evans, 2020
[20] "The Camera," 2009

upper atmosphere with the replacements, scientists cringed to see the new camera shake and rattle all the way. The actual installation took 35 hours of spacewalks, starting on December 3, 1993. Instructions to the astronauts were to fix everything that needed fixing since the cost of each trip was so exorbitant. Two rate-sensor units were replaced after half of the gyroscopes failed. The solar arrays were next. The first rolled smoothly into the storage canister, but the second balked at a bent strut, which was reluctantly cast overboard. The Wide Field and the Planetary cameras were both updated in the hope that they would assist in the elimination of blur.

The WFPC 2 was formerly a ground-based unit but seemed to adapt as anticipated, and an optical corrector was upgraded. On the fifth day, COSTAR was slotted in, replacing the overheating solar array drive electronics. Several weeks were required in which to fully align the telescope with its new parts.

Astronauts had no way of knowing if the new photos would be a marked improvement. On the ground, champagne flowed and tears fell as the first images came in with spectacular quality. More snags were to follow over the next 15 years, but the teams and designers grew more adroit at meeting each new quirk. Despite a seemingly fatal flaw at the very heart of its mission, Hubble would henceforth go on to make a series of startling achievements despite its temporarily compromised mirror.

Producing Results

For all of the difficulties involved in designing the telescope, which required contracting with several different companies, using the telescope is quite easy. The Hubble telescope has its own operations center, the Space Telescope Science Institute (STScI), which is the sole operator of the telescope. The STScI, which has a staff of hundreds of scientists, engineers, and astronomers, operates the telescope mostly on behalf of NASA and also sometimes for the European Space Agency, but it also operates the telescope for amateur astronomers too.

Since the telescope was originally supposed to launch in the early '80s, NASA had already formulated certain projects for the telescope several years before it actually launched. These projects immediately took precedence and needed a substantial amount of time to complete. Among the first projects was the development of the Hubble Constant, discussed further in Chapter 5.

Each year, the STScI will set out an annual schedule for using the telescope, which is accomplished by receiving and reviewing requests for where to aim the telescope and what to point it at. Most of the requests come from NASA or the European Space Agency, and the STScI works closely with both space agencies to develop ideas for using the telescope. Individual projects, which can be proposed by any member of the public, are also included.

Once the STScI knows what the Hubble will take images of for the year, it uses software to make a workable schedule for all of the projects that will take place. The STScI then has other software to control and monitor all of the telescope's instruments, giving it control of the telescope's flight. The operation of the telescope is synchronized with the schedule, but if an unpredictable event is in progress, the telescope can be adjusted quickly, as was the case in 2009 when an untracked and unrecorded asteroid slammed into Jupiter.

The HST is linked to the Tracking and Data Relay Satellite System, a combination of satellites in orbit and communications links on the surface. In addition to using this system to operate the telescope, the STScI relies on the system to receive the image data from the telescope.

When the telescope's images are transmitted through the system, the data goes to both the STScI and NASA. STScI feeds the data into algorithm software that analyzes everything and stores it.

The most unique aspect of the telescope is that any member of the general public can use it. In addition to conducting public outreach programs, the STScI has a process that allows amateur astronomers to send in applications proposing that the telescope be used for a project of their choosing.

Of course, it's not as simple as asking the STScI to look at an object. The proposal is subjected to peer-review by the STScI, so the applicant must have a pretty good idea what they're doing. The peer-review will determine whether the proposal is a worthwhile use of the telescope's time, but in any given year, the STScI will accept around 100 individual proposals.

When an applicant's proposal is selected, the STScI assists them by giving them software that will let the applicant determine how and where the telescope should point to do the project. Once the applicant figures it out with the STScI's special program, he or she can coordinate everything with the STScI, which will then operate the telescope and perform the project.

The telescope's original target, the bright Star Cluster 3532, 1,300 light years away, eventually received its due attention. It resides in the constellation of Carina, as the keel of the ship *Argo*. Informally known as the Wishing Well Cluster, it is said to resemble silver coins dropped into a well. Still, others have dubbed it the Football Cluster, which can be seen by the naked eye in the southern hemisphere. The cluster is 300 million years of age, but iconic photos of the nebulae are not likely to be a Hubble shot, given its troubled early months. A popular photo was taken by the Wide Field instrument at Chile's La Silla Observatory 23 years later.

In August 1990, Hubble came within a 0.1 arcsecond of analyzing the ring of material around the remnants of Supernova 1987A. By October, the first academic paper on Hubble had been submitted by Tod Lawes of the National Optical Astronomy Observatory in Tucson, Arizona.

The topic centered around the environment of black holes, still a theoretical concept inherited from Einstein and others.

Two weeks into 1991, Hubble accurately measured the distance to a neighboring galaxy, and the telescope provided a bonus in the process by investigating the Large Magellanic Cloud, a satellite of the Milky Way and the supernova's home. The viewing position in orbit around the Earth was a distance of 169,000 light years from the target. Two months later, Hubble's first images of Jupiter were released, featuring the "Giant Red Spot." In the view of the Jovian weather, the red dot is thought to be one or more large hurricanes to which warmer gases carry ammonia crystals from deep inside the atmosphere into the upper cloud layer. Through further observation, the oval shape of the dot has given way to a circular formation.

The ability of such a telescope to detect ancient entities was demonstrated in January 1992, when astronomers detected the rare element boron in an old star, a sign of the early universe. The 7th magnitude star resides 100 light years away. Boron is produced by high speed and energetic cosmic rays by supernovae. The "boron" star could be "fossil" evidence of events accompanying the birth of the Milky Way. Its discovery could force some modifications to the Big Bang Theory, appearing only in the ultra-violet range. The Big Bang may have already created some structures within the first minutes, including boron and beryllium.

In pursuit of black holes as tangible entities, Hubble was able to discover fuel being pulled into the abyss's gravitational center of galaxy NG4261 on November 19, 1992. The giant elliptical galaxy was 100 million light years away. A dust spiral 800 light years from Earth fuels the black hole toward the constellation of Virgo. The measured speed of swirling gas suggests a process 1.2 billion times the mass of the Sun.

On June 8, 1993, the new telescope tackled one of the most elusive questions asked in astronomical circles: the age and size of the universe. From the search came what is called the Hubble Constant, a unit of measurement used to describe the expansion of the universe. The initial rate has been established at 160 kilometers per second in every million light years of distance. The rate comes with a 10% uncertainty caveat. In this observation, Hubble targeted two "variable stars." Two fields were monitored, with exposures every 22 minutes over a period of 14 months.

Scientists once believed that the rapidly expanding universe was by now slowing considerably and that the velocity created by the Big Bang had lost much of its impetus. However, through the study of supernovae, stars that self-destruct in their final cycle of life, Hubble confirmed that the opposite is true. The universe continues to expand at an increasing rate as it has for billions of years. Such a realization points to the existence of "dark matter." For all that we do not understand about this invisible force, we can now see that it exceeds the force of gravity.

The dimensions of the universe are on the mind of any scientist or student who has pondered the nature of creation, beginning with whether it is infinite. If not, is there a distinct border where all that is known or can be sensed ends? The temptation to go further by guessing at what exists on the other side of that barrier is irresistible. Visualizing the totality as something that reconnects with itself, creating a contained infinity, has been considered.

These inquiries are premature, as astronomers are only given the "observable universe" as a model, which can best be found in Hubble's archival exploration. The telescope's ability to provide sharper images of distant galaxies and other objects in deep space was utilized shortly after the telescope was fixed in 1993. In a 10 day span during December 1995, the telescope was pointed at a region within the constellation Ursa Major, using a mixture of long exposure times and short exposure times to capture an image of objects in deep space.

This project, which came to be called Hubble Deep Field, provided a clear enough image for astronomers to locate thousands of different galaxies, comprised of different shapes. Moreover, some galaxies appeared to be in the process of colliding with each other. By using other measurements captured by other observatories, it was determined that some of the galaxies in the image were about 12 billion light years away, suggesting stars were forming within a few billion years of the Big Bang.

What made the Hubble Deep Field such an astonishing image is that it only covered about 0.000002 percent of the sky, or 1/500,000th. In other words, the image suggested that the universe consisted of tens of billions of galaxies. The telescope was used to take a similar image, referred to as Hubble Deep Field South, which showed similar results in a different part of the sky.

The telescope has since been used to take similar images that could look even further into deep space, including the Hubble Ultra Deep Field, captured from September 2003-January 2004. This image included galaxies that were created within a few hundred million years of the Big Bang, sharply reducing the length of time it took for stars to form after the Big Bang. This image was also able to capture and image individual stars nearly 60,000 light years away.

A 2018 picture of galaxies taken by the Hubble telescope

In addition to giving astronomers an idea about the sheer size of the universe, the images indicated the universe was "homogenous," meaning that the same physical principles applied everywhere. This was confirmation of a "cosmological principle" long held by astronomers that the Milky Way galaxy's position in the universe is not unique or somehow special.

At present, Hubble's modeling of the universe is comprised of an area 93.3 billion light years in diameter. Certainly, much more "universe" exists, and scientists are not helpless in calculating the possibilities. Employing the Bayesian Theory, a mathematical formula of probability, the force of an anticipated outcome presses against the unknown with the force of pre-existing evidence. In determining the dimensions of all that is, the Bayesian approach estimates a universe 250 times that of Hubble's 93.3 billion light years, a total of seven trillion light years in diameter.

The universe is gigantic, but with billions of large galaxies, sometimes they come into contact with each other. The Hubble telescope has captured images of galaxies "colliding" with each other. The collision occurs due to the gravitational pull of the galaxies upon each other, which may result in a merger of the two galaxies or the "cannibalization" of the smaller galaxy by the larger one.

Hubble has retrieved its imagery and data based not only on linear distance but on time. Present measurements are translated to the light year, the distance an object travels for one year at the speed of light. From "here to there" is entangled with from "then to now." The light Hubble receives is seen as it was in the past, depending on how far away the telescope is probing. The HTS has viewed galaxies so faint and distant that the images hearken back almost to the Big Bang. Discoveries have moved our observational clocks back to a time only a few hundred million years after that seminal event. According to Massimo Stiavelli of the Space Telescope Science Institute, "Hubble takes us to within a stone's throw of the Big Bang itself."[21]

The early galaxies show the chaos of the first moments of creation in contrast to the spirals so familiar to the modern-day. Every sort of shape is evident, such as the "toothpick" or "bracelet" configuration. From these earliest conditions, Hubble receives about one photon per minute, a mere trickle compared to later galaxies, which we receive at approximately 1,000,000 per minute. Searching so far back toward the beginning of observable time, the faintest of the earliest galaxies reach observers here with a brightness level one-tenth of a billion less than the human eye can detect. The stars that can be photographed with the Hubble's superior optics are those bodies described as the "second generation," after the first examples of matter made by the new universe. This is enabled by a camera no larger than a phone booth, capturing light sent out from the center of the universe long before the Earth came into existence.

Similarly, people on Earth have long believed that the solar system began as a disc. Hubble reveals how prolific such a pattern is in the creation of young stars and their surrounding bodies. In the Orion nebula, half of the young stars are surrounded by gas and dust structures in the early stages, many of them discs.

With such a history of pursuing the question, we suspect the universe accelerates through the poorly understood phenomenon of dark matter. Astronomers regularly release new data on how supernovae have changed over time. The more distant the exploding stars, the fainter they are, time-stretched accordingly (red-shifted). The accelerating universe, according to scientists such as Neal deGrasse Tyson, represents the likely end of the universe, in which all atomic and molecular matter, biological and inert, come unbound and fall away.

In mid-January of 1994, Hubble released data on its observations of Eta Carinae, a massive, unstable star. Prone to violent outbursts, "Carina" is 4 million times brighter than the Sun and 150 times more massive. Over a century ago, it was among the brightest stars in the sky, despite its distance. What Hubble observed was the last gasp of the dying star, 7,500 light years away, losing its essential materials in a massive wind of charged particles in the constellation Carina. The mass lost equals one Sun every thousand years, and the expected outcome is that the spent star will explode within a million years.

[21] "Hubble Digs," 2007

Barely four months later, black holes took center stage as observations targeted elliptical galaxy M87 at 50,000,000 light years. A supermassive black hole was confirmed at the galactic center, a "gravitationally collapsed object with rapid rotation at its core."[22] This provided seemingly conclusive evidence of previously theoretical entities predicted 80 years ago by Einstein's Theory of Relativity. The inner matter weighs as much as 3 billion Suns concentrated into a space no larger than the solar system. Through the years, observations of flaring have been recorded as sudden upticks in brightness as the phenomenon interacts with the materials around it.

Many around the world remember the comet that struck Jupiter, covered on the evening news in 1994. Multiple fragments of comet Shoemaker-Levy 9 serially impacted Jupiter's atmosphere over a period of days. In the first recorded case of two such astronomical objects colliding, the Jovian atmosphere was described as being "bruised" by the comet's entry.

First discovered by Carolyn and Gene Shoemaker and David Levy, Shoemaker-Levy had likely orbited Jupiter for over a decade before being captured and torn apart by its gravity. Each fragment produced a stunning impact with the force of 300,000,000 atomic bombs. Gas plumes were sent upwards of 300,000 kilometers, and the heated atmosphere reached 71,000 degrees Fahrenheit.

----

[22] Garner, 2021

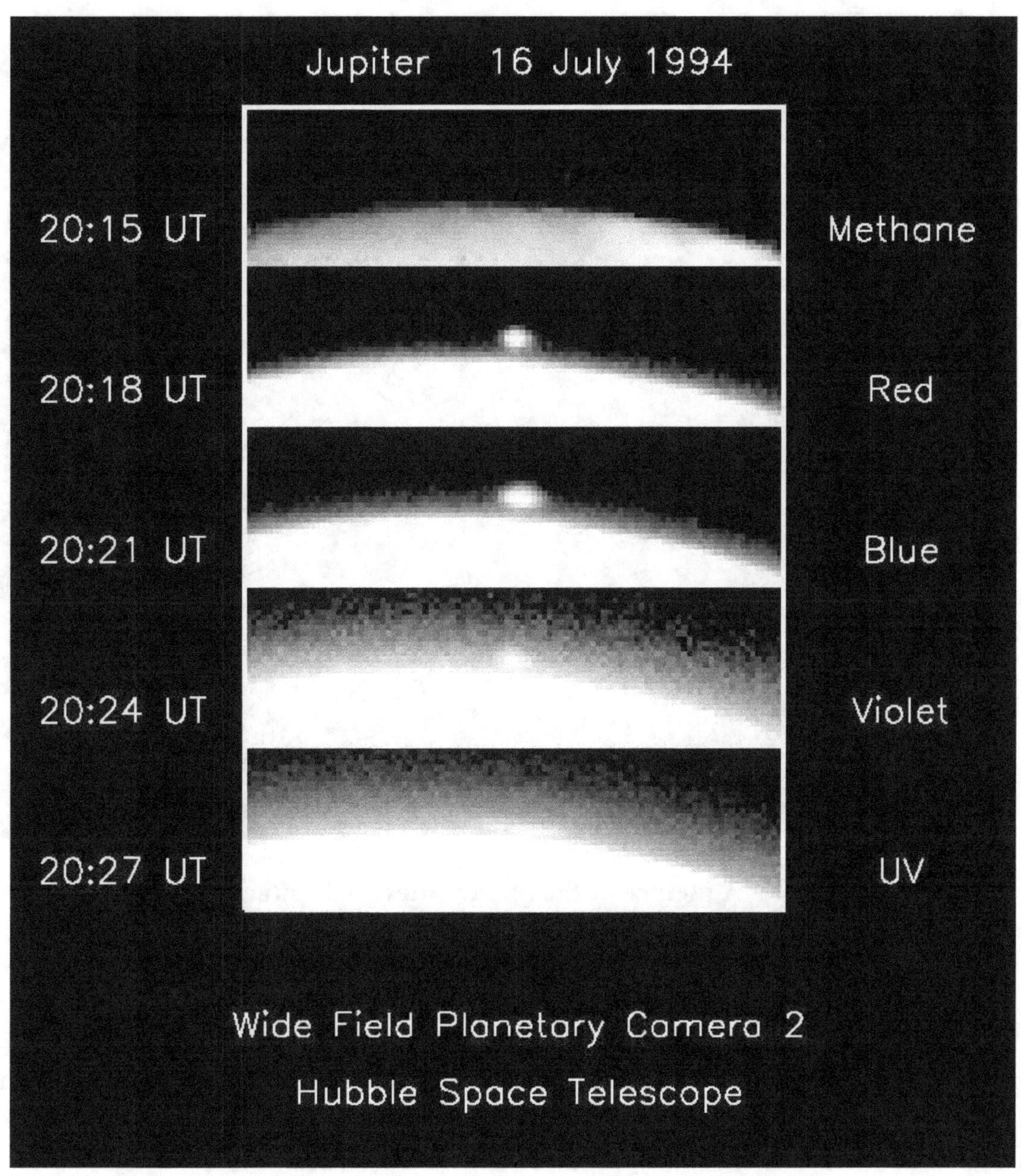

Hubble telescope pictures of the impact

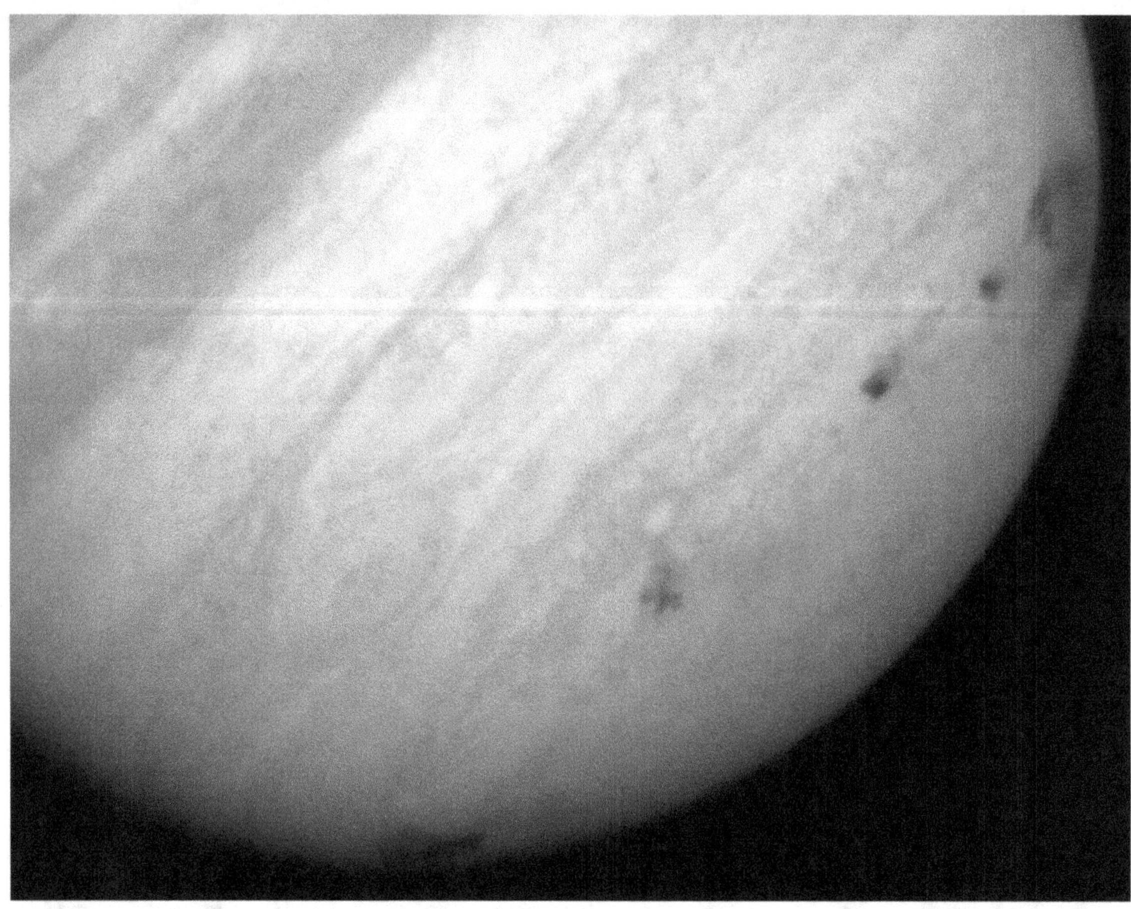

A picture of the impact sites on Jupiter

By November, Hubble had moved on to investigate the surface features of Saturn's moon Titan, a topic of much interest. Larger than Mercury but smaller than Mars, Titan's atmosphere is four times denser than that of Earth, with nitrogen as its primary component. The hazy moon was mapped by bright and dark surface features in a 16-day rotation, with one prominent, bright area being the size of Australia. Titan was, at the time, the only body in the solar system outside of the Earth with confirmed oceans. They are, however, predominantly comprised of ethane and methane, and the surface liquid is frozen harder than granite. Hubble employed its Wide Field Planetary Camera 2 (WFPC 2) in the infrared wavelength, producing 14 "noise-free"[23] images, free from signal interference. In all, 50 images were produced, and the data was to be of great importance to the Cassini Mission as it entered Saturn's region.

Hubble returned to Jupiter by February 1995, encountering oxygen on the surface of Europa, making the moon only the third object in the solar system to have some. That said, Europa holds a "tenuous atmosphere"[24] in which the surface pressure measures one hundred billionth that of

---

[23] Greicius, 2013

[24] "Hubble Finds," 2005

Earth. If all the oxygen were compressed on the surface, it would fill no more than a dozen Houston Astrodomes. Hubble's ability to detect such a small amount is impressive, but caution must be taken to avoid misinterpreting the presence of oxygen as a sign of life. November was taken up with star births in the Eagle Nebulae, nicknamed the Pillars of Creation. Located in the constellation of Serpens, it was discovered by Swiss astronomer Phillipe Loys de Chéveaux in the mid-18th century and more completely viewed by Messier in 1764, who dubbed it M16. "Eagle" measures 70 light years by 55 light years and contains several regions suited to the creation of stars. Within the visible clouds of hydrogen, gravity pulls clouds of gas together to collapse inward. If enough gas is present, nuclear fusion ignites the center. The data on star formation is essential to our knowledge of the early universe. The nebula is visible to low-power telescopes or binoculars, and the iconic Hubble photos have inspired much amateur activity.

Composite images of the previously unknown areas of the universe were released on January 15, 1996, known as the "Deep Field," in which exposures of 342 minute portions of the sky were taken from WFPC 2 over ten consecutive days. The composite images show a group of 1,500 galaxies at various stages of development from a narrow "keyhole" that goes far back in time, all from an area the size of a dime at 75 feet away. Most exposures taken the month before release revealed galaxies four billion times fainter than what the human eye can detect. These ancient entities were never seen by ground telescopes—one astronomer described the composite images as "deep core samples,"[25] the astronomical equivalent of the Dead Sea Scrolls.

Two days later, new data showed evidence of a planet orbiting the star Beta Pictoris. The hidden object had been blocked by an inner region of dust and warped by the new planet's gravitational pull.

In early March 1996, observations of the dwarf planet Pluto revealed basins and impact craters on the surface. These were detected through the study of brightness variations in blue light. Nearly all of Pluto's surface was imaged in its rotation of 6.4 days, and it was shown to be a complex object. The exposures were taken with the ESA's Faint Object Camera. Pluto's size equates to roughly two-thirds of Earth's moon, only 12,000 times farther away. One scientist compared the imaging of the small sphere to "read[ing] the small printing on a golf ball thirty-three miles away."[26]

The Hubble Space Telescope took its 100,000[th] exposure on June 22, 1996, and the subject was a quasar that resides nine billion light years from Earth. Before the use of the Hubble telescope, astronomers were baffled as to the nature of "quasi-stellar radio sources," better known as quasars, which were incredibly bright objects billions of light years away. In fact, these quasars were emitting incredibly powerful amounts of energy across the electromagnetic spectrum,

---

[25] Williams, 1996

[26] "The Surface of Pluto," 1998

brighter and more powerful than galaxies. However, astronomers couldn't determine the size or nature of the quasars.

Astronomers only recently began to figure out what these quasars are after the Hubble telescope pinpointed their locations at the centers of galaxies. It turned out a quasar is the nucleus of an active galaxy with a supermassive black hole, which is pulling in and devouring stars near it. As these stars get closer, some of its material is stripped away and begins to form an "accretion disc" around the center of the galaxy. The black holes don't emit light, but the accretion disc begins to emit incredible amounts of light and energy as they draw nearer to the black holes, eventually heating up to millions of degrees Fahrenheit. The light emitted from this relatively small area can outshine hundreds of galaxies that hold billions of stars. Despite the fact the Milky Way is 100,000 light years across, it is not a large enough galaxy to have a supermassive black hole capable of creating one of these quasars.

The telescope also taught astronomers considerably more about gamma-ray bursts. Scientists and astronomers have been able to identify and detect gamma-rays, the most radioactive emission on the electromagnetic spectrum, for over a century, but as soon as NASA started putting satellites in orbit, they began detecting gamma-ray flashes without having a clue where they originated.

Astronomers' understanding of gamma-ray bursts only developed in the 1990s by using the Hubble telescope's ability to capture images of gamma-ray bursts in conjunction with gamma-ray detectors like the Compton Gamma-Ray Observatory. Despite usually taking place billions of light years away, gamma-ray bursts are so bright that one in 2008 was visible to the naked eye. At the same time, most of the bursts only last about one second, and until March 2011, the longest lasting bursts ever observed had lasted only a few hours.

The long gamma-ray bursts seem to be the death throes of massive stars collapsing into black holes or supernovae, emitting more radiation in a few seconds than the Sun will generate in its lifetime. Furthermore, the bursts seem to be relatively narrow beams moving at nearly the speed of light. Astronomers still haven't been able to determine the source of the short gamma-ray bursts.

In March 2011, the Hubble telescope and other telescopes and gamma-ray detectors observed the longest lasting gamma-ray burst yet seen. This burst was still beaming bright emissions more than a week after detected, and when the HST zeroed in on the location it located a galaxy 3.8 billion light years away, with the emission coming from the galaxy's center. Astronomers believe this burst was the result of a massive star coming too close to the supermassive black hole at the center of the galaxy, which began stripping the star of its matter. The brightness and length of the burst suggests the gamma-ray burst was emitted in a direction toward Earth.

Sightings of gamma-ray bursts are rare partly because they are only visible when the emissions are beamed in certain directions. From Earth, many gamma-ray bursts will never be detectable, which is a good thing because if Earth was in the path of a long gamma-ray burst emitted even from thousands of light years away, it would destroy much of the atmosphere, instantly stripping about half of the planet's ozone layer. That said, the destruction of the ozone layer would no longer be a concern because the extreme amount of radiation emitted by these gamma-ray bursts would almost immediately kill all life on the planet, and snd since gamma-ray bursts are moving at almost the speed of light, there's no way to see it coming ahead of time.

The Hubble telescope's first image taken of a star's surface was a picture of Betelgeuse, a red supergiant in the Orion constellation nearing the end of its life. The behemoth has a radius of 600 million miles, 1,400 times that of the Sun and a billion times the volume. The exposure taken from 650 light years away in the ultra-violet wavelength featured a mysterious hot spot on the surface. In this location, temperatures reach 2,000 Kelvin above all other areas.

The second servicing mission for the telescope was performed from February 11-21, 1996. The most important upgrades involved the installation of two new technologically advanced instruments: the combination Near Infrared Camera and Multi-Object Spectrometer (NICMOS), which allowed Hubble to view the universe in infrared; and the Space Telescope Imaging Spectrograph (STIS), which brought celestial objects into greater detail and was built for hunting black holes. Both instruments were calibrated for the flawed primary mirror, replacing the Goddard High-Resolution Spectrograph and the Faint Object Spectrograph. This technology was not available during the first years of the mission.

The upgrades proved their worth on May 12, 1997 by spectrographically recording the first signature of a black hole. Hubble mapped motions of gas caught in the gravitational pull at the center of the M84 Galaxy, and the gas within the black hole's grip was measured at velocities up to 8,000 miles per hour.

A plume of gas and dust was observed from a volcanic eruption on the innermost moon, Io, at a height of 2,500 miles when targeting Jupiter and its moons once more a month later. The blast initiated at 2,000 miles per hour, but on Io, the plume reached a far greater altitude than it would have on Earth because the atmosphere is comparatively thin and the weak gravity allows for little resistance.

Of all the inquiries that astronomers could make by reaching outside its world into space, finding the process by which the universe moves was paramount. Concrete preliminary evidence for an accelerating universe from five years earlier was confirmed by Hubble telescope in September 1998. With the extreme precision involved in the missions and the data from Hubble's few years aloft, old misconceptions of space were overthrown by this single observation.

A month later, NASA assembled a "host mission" for the purpose of validating the functionality of the new equipment on the next servicing mission within the working environment. The crew was transferred by the *Discovery* shuttle to the telescope with a familiar face aboard. Joining the mission was John Glenn, the third man in space and the first American to orbit the Earth.

The Ring Nebula was discovered 200 years ago by French astronomer Charles Messier, who cataloged it as Messier 57, or M57. On January 6, 1999, Hubble provided a view of the ring of which Messier could only have dreamed. Hubble catches a haze signifying the glowing remains of a sun-like star. What makes the ring unusual is that the interior is filled with material. The nebula is one light year across, and the ring wraps around a football-shaped structure that has exhausted its hydrogen supply. The inner-glow comes from interior radiation interacting with a mass of helium. In approximately 10,000 years, the image will grow fainter and meld into its environment since its partner star is not strong enough for an explosive finale.

Hubble entered safe mode as an automatic reflex following the failure of four out of six gyroscopes on November 13, 1999. It maintained its security by pointing itself to the Sun so the solar array would receive power and the antennae would function for communication with Earth. All scientific work was suspended for the protection of the remaining gyros, and the overall mission was not threatened. Three of the six gyros were older and had a history of trouble after 50,000 hours of service, but the newer ones were less susceptible. When the system was turned on again, there was an unusual noise in the electric system. When jogged again, it was found that the gyros were misreading the rates, acting as if something had occurred when it had not. In this state, nearby and fast-moving targets were difficult to track, but by December 19, the next service mission was conducted, and the gyros and a new computer were installed.

An odd announcement was released on May 3, 2000, stating that Hubble had located the universe's missing hydrogen. Masses of the element had been created by the Big Bang shortly after which it disappeared. Hydrogen should have been present in all subsequent galaxies. However, by studying the light of quasars passing through intertwining clouds of gas in transit, it was found in invisible filaments that wove their way between galaxies throughout the universe.

Astronomers have long looked for primal reserves of hydrogen, accounting for nearly half of "normal" matter in the universe. The rest is locked up in galaxies in an unrecognizable form. Hubble was, at first, unable to see it in the immense clouds in a hot and rarified state. Supercomputer models predict an intricate web of gas filaments where hydrogen is concentrated along vast chain-like structures, with galaxy clusters forming where the chains intersect.

Birthing chambers for planets abound as well, but as a rule, behind clouded curtains of dust and gas. On April 26, 2001, Hubble found the first direct visual evidence of planet growth. Planetary "building blocks"[27] reside within dusty disks of young stars in the Orion Nebula where they are "blowtorched"[28] by ultra-violet radiation from the region's brightest star, which makes planetary formation difficult. Young planets must "beat the clock" as dust grains stick together while stars try to tear them apart. The process has been likened to "building a skyscraper in a tornado."[29]

Detecting the first elements in an exoplanet's atmosphere occurred in a body-orbiting sun-like star, HD 209458, 150 light years away. A seventh magnitude star, sodium was detected in one of its planets. Hubble was never fine-tuned for seeking out gases one might expect in a life-sustaining atmosphere, and such a find might provide the first evidence of life beyond Earth in gas caused by living organisms.

During the Servicing Mission of March 1-12, 2002, the HTS was not the only unit with problems. A cooling system on shuttle *Columbia* malfunctioned. A flight rule stating that a shuttle with only one cooling system must return to Earth was bent, and the astronauts reached Hubble for a nearly two-week regiment in which the Hubble Space Telescope was brought into the 21st century with a new Advanced Camera for Surveys. The flexible solar arrays were replaced, bringing a 30% increase to the power supply. The power control unit was updated, and a new cooling system was installed for the Near Infrared Camera, which had depleted its cooling source, a 230-pound block of nitrogen ice. Spacewalkers replaced one of four reaction wheel assemblies. With the first technological improvements in over a decade, data work increased in speed 10 times over. The first images from the Advanced Survey Camera were revealed on April 30, 2002. They were not expected to be utterly pristine but valuable for focusing the camera. Exposures appeared somewhat fuzzy from atmospheric "smear," but they were clearer than ground-based shots of the same target.

In the Crab Nebula, Hubble captured the dynamics of a "tremendous stellar explosion"[30] in which matter and antimatter were propelled to nearly the speed of light. The remarkable look at the Crab Pulsar and the vast nebula it powers shows the remnants of a supernova from 900 years prior. The nebula is ten light years across and 7,000 light years from Earth in the constellation Taurus. The exposure was taken by the WFPC 2 at a wavelength of 550 nanometers.

••

[27] Garner, 2021

[28] Bally, Throop, and O'Dell, 2001

[29] Bally, Throop, and O'Dell, 2001

[30] Frommert and Kronberg, 2013

A mosaic of the Crab Nebula taken by the Hubble telescope

The *Columbia* was lost in a tragic reentry failure on September 19, 2002 after a 15- day mission, and the subsequent servicing mission was canceled. The Hubble maintenance schedule stalled as administrators and the federal government considered the shuttle program's future.

In March of the following year, Hubble encountered an evaporating planet. The "hot Jupiter"[31] giant gaseous planet HD 209458b was orbiting closely around its parent star, and the atmosphere bled at a rapid rate into space, with much of the planet disappearing and leaving only a dense core. It was the first recorded account of such a phenomenon. Planets such as this one, orbiting so close to their stars, are unable to endure at such short distances essentially melt. This one, only four million miles from its star, had a hot and "puffed up"[32] evaporating hydrogen atmosphere leaving a comet trail behind it in a tight, 3.5-day orbit. The planet's position was too close for Hubble to photograph it directly, but the imaging spectrum could be used when the planet partially blocked light from its star, and hydrogen emission dropped drastically at those times.

---

[31] "Hubble Discovers," 2003

[32] "Hubble Discovers," 2003

Also in March 2003, Hubble recorded a "light echo"[33] around star V8381, Monocertis. It suddenly swelled in brightness at 6 million times the luminosity of our sun, and the outburst showed through the dust clouds. It temporarily became the brightest star in the Milky Way, but faded back into near anonymity since. Hubble caught the most extreme light echo ever seen, like flashbulbs in the fog, and a detailed CAT scan-like view of the three-dimensional structure of dust shells surrounding the star was recorded. The capture gave scientists a recording of the star's unusual explosion 20,000 light years from Earth. Despite the distance, enough energy was released to highly illuminate the surrounding dust before being reflected to Earth on an indirect path, forcing it to take longer to reach people here.

A second patch of trouble uncomfortably similar to the mirror scare occurred in 2004. Among the most serious malfunctions befalling the Hubble in its early years involved the Space Telescope Imaging Spectrograph. The component that separates light beams into their constituent colors failed four years into the mission, as it would do again, several years later. A failure in the power supply required the replacement of a low-voltage supply circuit board. For this task, specialized tools were designed.

Few scientists have had the opportunity to study a comet collision up close, but on July 4, 2005, the NASA spacecraft *Deep Impact* intentionally created such a moment when it released an 820-pound projectile in the path of comet 9P/Temple 1. Hubble's observation, including before and after exposures, clearly shows that Temple 1 appeared four times brighter than before, with an inner cloud of dust and gas surrounding the entity, increasing 200 kilometers in size. After 62 minutes of gas and dust ejection, the debris field expanded outward in a fan-shape, traveling at 1,800 kilometers per hour.

■■■

---

[33] "Hubble Watches," 2003

A picture of the collision

Wear and tear on the gyroscopes meant imminent mechanical failure, so Hubble operations were moved to a two-gyro system to protect a third's longevity on August 31, 2005, and the observational life of the Hubble telescope was extended into 2008 by eight months. The use of two gyros instead of three gyros—which form the heart of the pointing system—was indistinguishable in terms of performance. The Hubble telescope needs to know its location as it completes each observation, preparing to seek its next target, and the three gyros once supplied that data, but the task was transferred to the Fixed Head Trackers instead.

While focusing on Pluto on October 31, 2005, two small moons of the dwarf planet were discovered by the telescope. Both wobbled erratically, and if one were able to stand on the surface, s/he could not have determined the time of sunrise. This "cosmic dance with a chaotic rhythm"[34] was undoubtedly caused by Pluto and Charon whirling around one another in a constantly shifting gravitational field. The moons' football shape strengthened the effect of "tumbl[ing] erratically."[35] The colors were surprising, as Kerberos was dark like a charcoal

---

[34] Chou, 2015

briquette, while the others were bright like sand.

Two months later, moons and Saturn-like dust rings around the planet Uranus were discovered. Named Mab and Cupid, the two moons' orbits had changed significantly over previous decades. Two unseen dust rings revealed bright clouds and a high-altitude haze above the south pole. The shots were taken by WFPC 2, the only time such detail had been seen since the *Voyager* spacecraft flyby.

The Hubble telescope observed a comet's impact with the Sun from April 18-20, 2006. Comet 73/P/Schwachmann-Wachmann 3 broke into fragments as it approached the Sun. On its final approach, the fragments were named alphabetically. Hubble caught fragments B and G shortly after major outbursts of activity, and the chunks were pushed down by tail outgassing in the same way astronauts maneuver with jetpacks. The comet's demise was a well-ordered "hierarchical destruction"[36] in which the less massive chunks accelerated away from the parent nucleus faster. Cometary nuclei are deep-frozen relics of the early solar system.

While science has not yet put a final definition to the nature of dark matter, Hubble did provide further proof of its existence on August 31, 2006. In cluster 0657-56, informally known as the Bullet Cluster, the Hubble Space Telescope witnessed a collision between two large cluster galaxies. Photos of hot gases in X-rays show two pink "clumps," containing most of the "normal" matter (baryonic). However, as hot gases pass through one another, almost all else is "blue." The dark matter is not slowed down by the collision and does not interact with itself, gas, or normal matter unless gravity is in play.

Unpredictable behavior in comets continued to surprise observers who relied on the telescope. A "mystery comet" was observed on October 29, 2007 that suddenly brightened a millionfold over a 24-hour period. It carried a tail of 400,000 miles and lingered near the Trojan asteroids - remnants of an early system - around Jupiter. It was the first time a new one had been found in that region. The rogue comet came from a family known as Centaurs, ice bodies found between Jupiter and Neptune. Its eventual fate could include being pulled into Jupiter or the Sun. If ejected from the system, it could go on as an interstellar comet.

Toward the end of 2007, a hazy extrasolar atmosphere was discovered around a planet orbiting a distant star. The planet, HD 189733b, possessed carbon dioxide, the first time it was seen in the atmosphere of another star system. An important chemical signal for possible extraterrestrial life, the planet was too hot for any recognizable form. Earlier observations found water vapor and methane in the atmosphere. However, carbon dioxide was of the greatest interest to those searching for connections to biological life.

------

[35] Chou, 2015

[36] "Hubble provides," 2006

More "firsts" were in store on March 8, 2008, when an organic molecule was detected in an exoplanet's methane atmosphere, the first case of it outside the solar system. Using spectroscopy to split light to reveal fingerprints of various chemicals was a "crucial stepping-stone"[37] to assessing pre-biotic molecules where life can exist. Further observations flatly confirmed, "there is water."[38] The location is 63,000,000 light years away in the Vulpecula constellation ("the little fox"). The planet is another of the "hot Jupiter" type, so close to the parent star that orbiting takes one to two days, and its temperature is 900 degrees Centigrade.

The Hubble telescope marked 100,000 orbits of the Earth on August 11, 2008. By then, the telescope had spent two decades aloft, traveling at five miles per second and completing 2.72 billion miles, a distance that equals 5,700 round trips to the Moon. The day's work included turning the camera to the Tarantula Nebula near Star Cluster NGC 2074, 170,000 light years from Earth.

A Hubble telescope panorama of a star cluster in the Tarantula Nebula

Visible light images of an exoplanet orbiting the Fomalhaut star were released in November of that year. The star system lies 25 light years from Earth, and the target planet - a visible light source near the constellation Piscis Australio - was named Fomalhaut B. Searching there made sense for the potential for exoplanet analysis. However, Fomalhaut B threw Hubble a curve, fading away and vanishing in the later exposures. Red flags were raised when the entity failed to exhibit the behavior of an authentic planet. It may have been a cloud masquerading as a planet, or a collision might have removed it. The orbit seemed unusual to the point of eccentricity, and it offered no infrared signature.

The most recent service mission occupied a 12-day period in May 2009. After several delays, the shuttle *Atlantis* delivered a seven-member crew to the HTS to install the Cosmic Origins Spectrograph (COS) and WFPC3, plus a new science computer. A guidance sensor was refurbished, new insulation was provided to three electronics bays, and a device was attached to the base of the telescope to facilitate de-orbiting upon decommissioning. Amid minor repairs was the replacement of six aging batteries.

The lens returned to the asteroid belt in February of 2010, pointed at the asteroid Vesta, the second-largest object between Mars and Jupiter. A piece of Vesta fell in a fireball over Australia 30 years before Hubble's launch. In terms of girth, Vesta, visible to the naked eye, is only surpassed by Ceres, classified as a dwarf planet. It neared Earth four years earlier, at which time Hubble mapped its topographical surface and features to learn that it spans 530 kilometers across and sports a crust of cooled lava covering a rocky mantle. The core is comprised of iron and nickel, and lava once flowed several kilometers deep. An unusual amount of hydrogen was present, and highly reflective patches from its earliest years, from when it had liquid water, can be seen.

In 2011, Hubble's attention returned to dark matter, now recognized as the force taking the universe apart. With massive galaxy clusters acting like magnifying lenses in space, Hubble constructed a sharp map of dark matter in the universe. The Abell 1689 galaxy cluster lay 2.2 billion miles away, containing 1,000 galaxies and trillions of stars. Hubble used 135 lensed images of 42 background galaxies to calculate the location and amount of dark matter, then superimposed a map of infrared dark concentrations, tinted blue. The cluster was endowed with ample dark matter from its formation and has carried much of it along since.

Major projects were added to the Hubble agenda, including the Cluster Lensing and Supernova Survey. Over a three-year period, 25 clusters with high X-ray emissions were slated for analysis. X-ray emissions signify a great quantity of hot gas, further indicating that the clusters are massive. Hubble set out to map the dark matter distribution and seek more evidence of early cluster formation.

By July 4, 2011, Hubble was well into 1,000,000 science observations. On that day, the HTS searched for water in the atmospheres of exoplanets 1,000 light years away. The millionth exposure was taken of HAT-P-7b, a gas giant larger than Jupiter orbiting a star hotter than the sun. So reliant was the astronomy world on the HTS that by December of the same year, the ten-thousandth Hubble science paper was published.

Among the weightier subjects was an analysis of the Andromeda Galaxy around May 31, 2012. Andromeda is on a collision course with the Milky Way, and the impending merger will be profound. The Milky Way contains billions of stars across 100,000 light years of space. By the same token, Andromeda is far larger, double our diameter, with a trillion stars, locally, the most massive and luminous galaxy. The stars in the central bulge are rich in heavy metals. Where our ancient galaxies tend to be older at over 13 billion years, Andromeda has stellar streams six to eight billion years of age, signifying that an act of cosmic cannibalism has taken place. It is vast and far away, but Hubble has photographed a 61,000 light year stretch and assembled it into a mosaic photo of 7,398 exposures from 411 individual pointings. The composite image is a product of the Panchromatic Hubble Andromeda Treasury (PHAT) Program.

Hubble returned to Pluto on July 11, 2012, discovering a fifth moon around the dwarf planet. The new orbiter was a mere six to 15 miles across in an irregularly shaped diameter. The track sits at an average distance of 29,000 miles in a series of "nested" orbits. The fourth moon was discovered one year prior as the New Horizon spacecraft prepared for a flyby.

The latest composite image to show the entire cosmic history from one patch of sky was released on September 25, 2012 as the Hubble Extreme Deep Field (XDF). The first look showed what many of the first galaxies looked like in the visible spectrum, some extant shortly after the "dark ages." This was the period between the first emission of cosmic background and the time at which the evolution of structure in the universe led to the gravitational collapse of objects, forming the stars. Hubble shows the universe at only a few percent of its current age, and the Advanced Camera Survey and WFPC3 took the images in a combined effort, lasting over a decade.

Celebrating its 23rd year in space, the telescope examined the Horsehead Nebula on April 13, 2013, a small part of a star-forming complex in the Orion constellation, with an estimated disintegration in 5,000,000 years. The "Horsehead" is difficult to see with a personal telescope, but the Hubble shot in infrared is popular with the public. A dark molecular cloud residing 1,500 light years away, is formally classified as Barnard 33.

The Horsehead Nebula

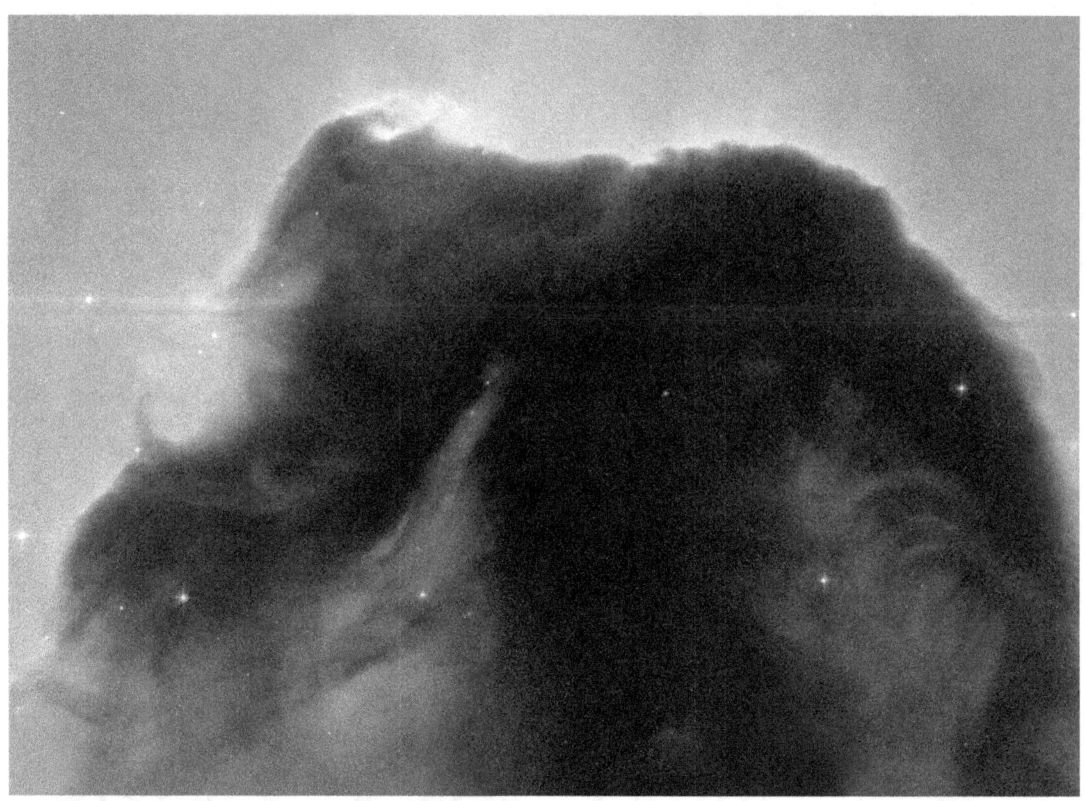

A picture of dust within the nebula taken by the Hubble telescope

The latter months of 2013 included an asteroid analysis in November, in which the main body trailed six comet-like tails behind it. However, December was even more important because water vapor plumes were discovered on Jupiter's Europa in the frigid south polar region. Previous analyses had pointed to a possible ocean under Europa's crust. If a connection to sub-surface activity is confirmed, scientists can directly investigate potentially habitable environments without drilling through the ice. Also noted by the Cassini mission, the Hubble telescope was pushed to its limits to see such a faint emission. The moon's long, fractured cracks, called *lineae,* may also indicate water vents. However, at its closest points to Jupiter, it does not vent. This may signify a tidal flex below as the plumes fall back to the surface at an altitude of 125 miles.

The next installment in the composite image histories was released on January 7, 2014. It featured galaxy cluster Abell 2744 in a multi-year program, probing the super-deep field with long exposures. These included some of the faintest ever taken. Dubbed the First Frontier Field Image, it was shown at that year's meeting of the American Astronomical Society in Washington, D.C. Abell 2744 contains several hundred galaxies as they appeared in the early universe. The immense gravity in background clusters was used as "gravitational lensing,"[39]

---

[39] "Hubble's First," 2014

which warps space, brightening and magnifying old distant galaxies.

The composite is also an experiment, testing whether we can use Hubble's exquisite quality and Einstein's Theory of Relativity to reach the first galaxies. Some of the 3,000 backgrounds are ten to 20 times larger than they would normally appear. Without gravitational lensing, the image would be "smeared," stretched, and duplicated across the field. Hubble can see dwarf galaxies at 01.100th the mass of the Milky Way. Plans are in place to view them again, but visible and infrared wavelengths will be switched for the second observation.

A disintegrating asteroid was first spotted by Hawaii's Keck Observatory and turned over to Hubble in March of 2014. The asteroid was imaged as its fragments drifted apart at one mile per hour, eliminating collision as a cause. The ten fragments are further disintegrating. Typically, fragile ice and dust comets fall apart near the Sun, but one had not been observed doing so in the asteroid belt. The largest fragments were four football fields long. The reason for disintegration, since the Sun's worst heat was not near, may have been sunlight, causing an uptick in rotation with a weakness in the interior, which has occurred in other cases—the pieces succumb to centrifugal force and pull apart.

Changes in Jupiter's environment necessitated inclusion on Hubble's agenda in May 2014. The "Great Red Spot" appeared to be shrinking and changing in shape from oval to circular. Previously, the dot could house three Earths in its diameter, but it was now only one width of the smaller planet, only 10,250 miles across. The shape change has been attributed to small current eddies joining the storm.

New potential targets were scheduled for 2014 in the Kuiper Belt as a boost for the *New Horizons* spacecraft, preparing to leave Pluto behind. Hubble had imaged the surface where ground instruments could not. After the *New Horizons*, Hubble found another target for a flyby: after searching the deep sky, a tiny icy world was located within a region of similar bodies beyond Neptune's orbit. The combination of the Hubble Telescope and the space probe heading out at 32,800 miles per hour confirmed the previously unseen Ultima Thule.

Discovering the moons of Pluto before the arrival of *New Horizons* was timely. *New Horizons* would have discovered them as well, but only a few months prior to arrival with no time for preparation. Arrival at Ultima Thule was predicted for New Year's Day in 2015.

In mid-January, a panoramic view of the Andromeda Galaxy was released, a mosaic of 7,389 exposures including 100,000,000 stars and thousands of clusters, the largest ever such image.

The first predicted supernova was captured on December 6, 2015. It exploded in a galaxy behind a cluster, causing it to appear in different locations at different times. Timelapses of its spiral galaxy, NGC 2525, show the explosion and aftermath, with a white dwarf "slurping"[40] up material from a companion star and detonating in a thermonuclear blast. Located 70,000,000 light years away, the brightness and rate of fade in the event helped measure the distance.

The "Cosmic Distance Record" was broken again on March 3, 2016, when Hubble found a galaxy only 400 million years removed from the Big Bang. The bright infant GN-z11 as it was seen 13.4 billion years ago, was the most remote, besting the previous record of 13.2 billion. Considering the high brightness of the new galaxy suggests that "other unusually bright galaxies found in earlier photos are really at astonishing distances."[41]

A new moon was discovered orbiting the dwarf planet Makemake in the Kuiper Belt on April 26, 2016. The planet was named for a creation deity of the Rapa Nui people of Easter Island. Makemake is the second-brightest icy dwarf planet, and its orbiting moon is merely 100 miles across, 870 miles wide, and extraordinarily faint. The WFPC 3 employed the same process used for Pluto's moons.

While studying the atmosphere of exoplanets in February 2017, seven earth-like planets orbiting Trappist-1 were discovered. Several resided within a habitable zone according to the spectrographic survey. One lacks the puffy hydrogen clouds—hydrogen is a greenhouse gas that smothers planets orbiting too close to the parent star—of the others. The results favor the cloudless orbs with environments more aligned with Earth, Venus, and Mars.

On the same level as universal expansion and elements on exoplanets is the confirmation of gravitational waves 130 light years from Earth. These create ripples in space caused by violent, energetic events in the universe. Hubble observed the source of the resulting "kilonova,"[42] a stellar blast caused by the colliding of compact objects. Neutron stars can yield gold, plutonium, and other elements when they collide, theoretically generating gravitational waves, as well. The first such waves detected in October 2017 were accompanied by short gamma bursts from NCG 4993 at an enormous distance. The pulse of a powerful explosion of light was picked up around the world. It was the first time we had seen light and gravitational waves coming from the same event. The most distant star ever discovered was found in April 2018, named Icarus. Its starlight was magnified by intervening clusters of galaxies in the now-familiar process of gravitational lensing. The star's formal name is MACSJ1149+2223 Lensed Star 1. Through gravitation lensing, Icarus was the first case of seeing a "magnified individual star,"[43] according to Patrick Kelly of the University of Minnesota.

After viewing interstellar objects and phenomena, one finally visited our system on June 27, 2018. The first recorded interstellar object, Oamuamua, passed through the solar system,

---

[40] Torbet, 2020

[41] Rhodan, 2016

[42] Phillips, 2013

[43] Kooser, 2018

suddenly gaining an unexpected boost of speed. In this way, it acted comet-like, expelling gaseous materials. Discovered by the big telescope in Hawaii, its tracking was funded by the Near Earth Object Observations (NEOO), an organization tracking incoming threats. On September 17, it "slingshotted"[44] past the Sun at 196,000 miles per hour. The origin of the object is likely the constellation Vega. It varies in brightness by a factor of 10 as it rotates on its axis. No known asteroid or comet from the solar system has ever varied so widely.

On October 3, 2018, a possible exomoon was found outside the solar system larger than Neptune and accompanying a planet more massive than Jupiter. The planet orbits a sun-like star, 7,800 light years from Earth. This single moon is ten times more massive than all moons and rocky planets in our system combined. The discovery made an "extraordinary claim,"[45] and caution was advised. The data was turned over to Hubble, and 40 hours later, the impression was confirmed. The decisive next transit across the face of the planet began 78 minutes earlier than calculated, suggesting another planet "tugging" at it. A planet and moon orbiting each other could also be the cause. David Kipping of Columbia University observed that his team was "unable to find any other single hypothesis which can explain all the data we have."[46]

The final chapter of the Hubble composites was completed in May 2019 and labeled the Deep Field Image Legacy. The patch of sky examined was nearly the size of a full moon. The image contains 7,500 exposures taken over 16 years and includes 265,000 galaxies and 13.3 billion years of cosmic history.

Hubble continues to work past its expected life span, well into the 21st century. On September 13, 2019, water vapor was discovered on an exoplanet in the habitable zone. The planet orbits a small red dwarf 110 light years away in the constellation of Leo. It may prove too extreme for humans, but hundreds of suitable "super-Earths"[47] are under consideration.

Galaxies are the best laboratories for studying the long-term environment, and Hubble himself once described galaxies as "markers of space."[48] From a lack of sufficient optics, weak computing power, and the absence of a delivery system, the Hubble telescope offers a present view to the beginning of time, space, and the beginning of life. Once thought to be impossible, scientists still receive photons from the beginning of time and space and possess the technology to image them.

When the Hubble Space Telescope was initially malfunctioning in 1990, nobody could have imagined that it would outlast the Space Shuttle Program. The space shuttles' versatility made it

---

[44] "Hubble Space Telescope," 2016

[45] Crockett, 2018

[46] Crockett, 2018

[47] "Hubble Space Telescope," 2019

[48] "Hubble Space Telescope," 2019

possible to perform many kinds of missions in orbit, from servicing the International Space Station to conducting scientific experiments for weeks at a time in orbit itself. The Hubble telescope was even designed with the space shuttles' abilities in mind, so that future space shuttle missions could repair and service the telescope.

However, budget concerns and a bad economy made NASA and space exploration the target of potential cuts during the 2010s, leading to uncertainty over America's space policy as a whole. NASA anticipated that the 2009 servicing mission of the telescope would be the last, and with the space shuttles being retired, there were no spacecrafts set to replace the space shuttles, so once they are retired, servicing missions to the HST are out of the question.

Without future servicing missions, it is not a question of if the Hubble telescope's equipment will malfunction but when. The telescope averaged a servicing mission almost once every three years, with equipment and instruments failing even more frequently, and while the telescope was equipped with state of the art instruments, orbiting around the Earth in space can be unforgiving on the delicate instruments, and the instruments must all complement each other properly for the telescope to function at its best. Furthermore, the telescope is projected to de-orbit the Earth and fall out of the sky within 20 years.

Better technology has allowed telescopes and observatories on the surface to see more, but NASA still intends to launch two more telescopes into orbit. The better-known telescope is the James Webb Space Telescope, named after NASA's administrator during the Apollo missions. That telescope will have better optics than the Hubble telescope, but its main advantage will be its infrared abilities. The Hubble telescope was never intended to maximize the use of infrared technology, although Wide Field Camera 3 was able to detect infrared rays. Infrared helps telescopes detect more stars in deep space. With better infrared abilities, the James Webb telescope is expected to be able to take even deeper images of space than the Hubble telescope.

The James Webb telescope or other telescopes may eventually be more powerful and capable than the Hubble telescope, but the Hubble telescope laid the groundwork for future deep space exploration and set the template for how to operate a space telescope. Newton once famously wrote, "If I have seen further, it is by standing on the shoulders of giants." After the publication of 15,000 academic papers based on the Hubble Space Telescope's investigations and its collection of superb photos, future missions will undoubtedly rely on the telescope's decades of data-gathering as primary sources.

Online Resources

Other books about space by Charles River Editors

Other books about the Universe on Amazon

Bibliography

A Hubble First: Water Vapor Found on Habitable Zone Exoplanet. (2019). Exoplanet Exploration, www.exoplanets.gov/news/1600/a-hubble-first-water-vapor-found-on-habitable-zone-exoplanet/.

About Hubble. (2021). ESA Hubble, www.esahubble.org/about.

Bally, J., H. Throop, and C. O'Dell. (2001). "Survivor" Planets: Astronomers Witness First Steps of Planet Growth—and Destruction. NASA: Hubblesite, https://hubblesite.org/contents/news-releases/2001/news-2001-13.html.

CCD Cameras: An Overview. (2021). Kisi, https://www.getkisi.com/guides/ccd-camera.

Chou, Felicia. (2015). Hubble Reveals That Two of Pluto's Moons Wobble Unpredictably, SciTech Daily, https://scitechdaily.com/hubble-reveals-that-two-of-plutos-moons-wobble-unpredictably/.

Crockett, Christopher. (2018). Hubble Boosts Case for Exomoon. Sky and Telescope, www.skyandtelescope.org/hubble-boosts-case-first-known-exomoon/.

Edwin Hubble: The Man Who Discovered the Cosmos. (2012). The European Space Agency, www.esa.int/About_Us/ESA_history/Edwin_Hubble-The-Man-Who_Discovered_The-Cosmos.

ESA/Hubble, M.Kornmesser, and L. Calçada. (2018). Hubble's Reaction Wheels. The European Space Agency, www.esahubble.org/videos/hubblecast114d/.

Europa. (2021). Europa Clipper, https://europa.nasa.gov/europa/ocean/.

Evans, Ben. (2020). What's wrong with the Hubble's mirror, and how was it fixed? BBC Sky at Night Magazine, https://www.skyatnightmagazine.com/space-missions/what-was-wrong-with-hubble-mirror-how-was-it-fixed/

Frommert, Hartmut and Christine Kronberg. (2013). The Missing Messier Objects. SEDS: The Messier Catalog, http://www.messier.seds.org/more/m001_hr.html.

Garner, Rob (Ed.). (2021). Hubble Space Telescope: About - Hubble History Timeline. NASA, https://www.nasa.gov/content/goddard/hubble-history-timeline.

Gough, Evan. (2019). Uh Oh, Hubble's Wide Field Camera 3 is Down. Universe Today, www.universetoday.com/141135.uf-oh-hubbles-wide-field-camera-3-is-down.

Greicius, Tony (Ed.). (2013). Hubble Space Telescope Sees Evidence of Water Vapor Venting off Jupiter Moon. NASA, https://www.nasa.gov/content/goddard/hubble-europa-water-vapor.

Haynes, Korey. (2019). Astronomers Stitch hits of hits into "Legacy Deep Field" Image. Astronomy, www.astronomy.com/news/2019/05/astronomers-stitch-hubbles-hits-into-legacy-deep-field-image.

Howell, Elizabeth, Hubble, Future Interstellar Comet? Gas-spewing object spotted in asteroid group near Jupiter, Space.com, March 2, 2021 – www.space.com/intersttellar-comet-nearJupiter-trojan-asteroids.

Hubble Astronomers Assemble Wide View of the Evolving Universe. (2019). Hubble—NASA, www.nasa.gov/feature/goddess/2019/hubble-astronomers-assemble-wide-view-of-the-evolving-universe.

Hubble Discovers and Evaporating Planet. (2003) Spaceflight Now, https://spaceflightnow.com/news/n0303/12planet/.

Hubble Finds Oxygen Atmosphere on Jupiter's Moon Europa. (2005). NASA: Europa Clipper, https://europa.nasa.gov/news/18/hubble-finds-oxygen-atmosphere-on-jupiters-moon-europa/.

Hubble finds universe's missing hydrogen. (2000). University of Wisconsin-Madison: News, www.news.wisc.edu/lost-and-found-hubble-finds-universes-missing-hydrogen/.

Hubble's First Frontier Field finds thousands of unseen, faraway galaxies. (2014). PHYSORG, https://phys.org/news/2014-01-hubble-frontier-field-thousands-unseen.html.

Hubble Overview. (2021). European Space Agency, www.esa.int/Science_Exploration_Science/Hubble_overview

Hubble provides spectacular view of ongoing comet breakup. (2006). ESA/Hubble, https://esahubble.org/news/heic0605/.

Hubble Sees Evidence of Water Vapor at Jupiter Moon. (2013). NASA Jet Propulsion Laboratory, www.jpl.nasa.gov/news/hubble-sees-evidence-of-water-vapor-at-jupiter-moon.

Hubble Space Telescope. (2016). NASA Science: Solar System Exploration, https://solarsystem.nasa.gov/missions/hubble-space-telescope/in-depth/.

Hubble Space-Telescope. (2019). NASA, https://www.nasa.gov/content/hubble-space-telescope-space-telescope-imaging-spectrograph.

Hubble Watches Light Echo from Mysterious Erupting Star. (2003). University of Arizona:
News, https://news.arizona.edu/story/hubble-watches-light-echo-mysterious-erupting-star.

Kooser, Amanda. (2018). NASA's Hubble Telescope snaps most distant star ever seen. CNET,
www.cnet.com/nasa-hubble-telescope-spots-most-distant-star-ever-seen-icarus/.

Loff, Sarah, (1990). Deployment of the Hubble Space Telescope. NASA,
www.nasa.gov/image-feature/april-25-1990-deployment-of-the-hubble-space-telescope.

McFadden, Christopher. (2021). A Brief History of the Telescope: From 1608 to Gamma-
Rays. Interesting Engineering, www.interestingengineering.com/a-brief-history-of-the-telescope-
from1608-to-gamme-rays.

Nave, R. (2005). "Expanding Universe." Hyperphysics, http://hyperphysics.phy-
astr.gsu.edu/hbase/Astro/hubble.html.

Paquin, K. (2008). Mission to Hubble. NASA,
www.nasa.gov/mission_pages/hubble/servicing/series/Hubble_space_armor.html

Phillips, Tony (Ed.). (2013). Hubble Sees the Fireball from a "Kilonova." NASA Science,
https://science.nasa.gov/science-news/science-at-
nasa/2013/03aug_kilonova#:~:text=August%203%2C%202013%3A%20NASA's%20Hubble,as
%20neutron%20stars%20crash%20together.

Rhodan, Maya. (2016). The Hubble Telescope Just Broke a New Cosmic Record. Time.
https://time.com/4248245/hubble-telescope-cosmic-record/.

Smith, Kiona N. (2018). How Astronauts Saved the Hubble Telescope from Disaster. Forbes,
https://www.forbes.com/sites/kionasmith/2018/04/25/how-astronauts-saved-the-hubble-space-
telescope-from-disaster/?sh=5432c84f5a33.

Spectrographs. (2020). NASA, www.nasa.gov/content/goddard/hubble-space-telescope-
science-instruments.

Summers, F. et al. (2015). Exploring the Hubble Extreme Deep Field. NASA: Hyperwall,
https://svs.gsfc.nasa.gov/30681.

"Survivor" Planets: Astronomers Witness First Steps of Planet Growth—and Destruction.
(2001). Hubblesite, www.hubblesite.org/contents/news-releases/2001/news-2001-13.html.

Swain, M. (2008). Hubble Finds First Organic Molecule on an Exoplanet. NASA: Hubblesite,
https://hubblesite.org/contents/news-releases/2008/news-2008-11.html.

The Camera That Saved Hubble…Twice: JPL's Wide Field and Planetary Camera 2. (2009). Jet Propulsion Laboratory, www.jpl.nasa.gov/news/the-camera-that-saved-hubble-twice-jpls-wide-field-and-planetary-camera-2.

Telescope History. (2003). NASA, www.nasa.gov/audience/forstudents/9-12/features/telescope_feature_912.html.

The Surface of Pluto. (1998). NASA: Jet Propulsion Laboratory, https://www.jpl.nasa.gov/images/the-surface-of-pluto.

The Telescope. (2021). Hubblesite, http://hubble.stsci.edu/the_telescope/nuts_.and._bolts/instruments/fgs/.

Thompson, R. (2021). Hubble's Near Infrared Camera Digs for Galactic Gold. The European Space Agency, www.esahubble.org/images/heic0406b.

Torbet, Georgina. (2020). Hubble captures a spectacular time-lapse of a supernova explosion. Digital Trends, www.digitaltrends.com/news/hubble-supernova-time-lapse/.

Wide Field Astro-Imaging, Part 1: The Gear You Need. (2013). 42 West, www.adorama.com/alc-wide-field-astro-imaging-part-1-the-gear-you-need.

Williams, R. (1996). Hubble's Deepest View of the Universe Unveils Bewildering Galaxies Across Billions of years. NASA: Hubblesite, https://hubblesite.org/contents/news-releases/1996/news-1996-01.html.

Wilson, Jim (Ed.). (2007). Hubble Digs Deeply, Toward Big Bang. NASA, www.nasa.gov/vision/universe/starsgalaxies/hubble_UDF.html.

Free Books by Charles River Editors

We have brand new titles available for free most days of the week. To see which of our titles are currently free, click on this link.

Discounted Books by Charles River Editors

We have titles at a discount price of just 99 cents everyday. To see which of our titles are currently 99 cents, click on this link.